GREAT DISASTERS

THE BLACK DEATH

JAMES DAY

Illustrated by
PATRICK BULLOCK
AND PETER BULL

The Bookwright Press
New York · 1989

Great Disasters

The Black Death
The Chernobyl Catastrophe
The Hindenburg Tragedy
The Eruption of Krakatoa
The Fire of London

The Attack on the Lusitania
The Destruction of Pompeii
The San Francisco Earthquake
The Space Shuttle Disaster
The Sinking of the Titanic

First published in the
United States in 1989 by
The Bookwright Press
387 Park Avenue South
New York, NY 10016

First published in 1989 by
Wayland (Publishers) Limited
61 Western Road, Hove
East Sussex BN3 1JD

© Copyright 1989
Wayland (Publishers) Ltd

Library of Congress Cataloging-in-Publication Data

Day, James
    The Black Death/by James Day; illustrated by
Patrick Bullock and Peter Bull.
        p.   cm.—(Great disasters)
    Bibliography: p.
    Includes index.
    Summary: Examines the origins, spread, and
effects of the bubonic plague in fourteenth-
century England and Europe, as well as the later
discovery of its cause and cure.
    ISBN 0-531-18235-5
    1. Plague—History—Juvenile literature.
[1. Black death. 2. Plague.]   I. Bullock, Patrick,
ill.   II. Bull, Peter, 1960-ill.   III. Title.
IV. Series.
RC172.D39   1989
614.5'732'0094—dc 19   88-37302
                                                CIP
                                                AC

Front cover   *A medieval woodcut showing the plague (the skeleton) cutting its way through a crowd of people like a farmer cuts through a crop of wheat.*

Words that are printed **bold** the first time they appear in the text are explained in the glossary.

Phototypeset by DP Press, Sevenoaks, Kent
Printed in Italy by G. Canale & C.S.p.A, Turin

CONTENTS

BISHOP'S WARNING

William of Edynton, the rich and powerful **Bishop** of Winchester, was watching workers toiling like ants up and down his great **cathedral**. The year was 1349, and they had been rebuilding the cathedral for four years now. Work was going well, but William was very worried as he looked on.

William had just received news that across the English Channel, where an English army was fighting the French, many people had already died from a terrible disease. He had heard that it had already killed half the **population** of France. There was no known cure, and now there were rumors that it had broken out in England. Nobody seemed to be taking it seriously. But what would happen if it broke out among his **clergy**, or his workmen?

Bishop William **(Below, left)** *dictates a letter to his priests to warn them of the plague. In the background you can see Winchester Cathedral being rebuilt.*

He decided that they had to be warned and wrote to his priests:

"The **plague** kills more viciously than a two-edged sword. Nobody dares enter any town, castle or village where it has struck. Everyone flees them in terror as they would the lair of a savage beast. There is an awful silence in such places; no merry music, no laughter. They have become dens of terror, like a wilderness. Where the countryside was fertile, it has now become a barren desert, for there is nobody to plow the fields. As I write this, my hand is trembling with fear; for the news I have to pass on to you is that this plague may have broken out in certain parts of our kingdom of England."

Bishop William's fears were to be proved right. Even as he was writing, men and women only seventy miles away, in the south coast port of Melcombe Regis, near Weymouth, were showing the **symptoms** of **bubonic plague**.

Left *Pilgrims going to Canterbury. During the time of the Black Death such trips became rare. Most people stayed where they were in order to avoid becoming infected with the plague.*

6

People who caught the plague first started to shiver, and then they became feverish. They began to sweat, cough up blood and vomit. Their heads, backs and limbs ached violently. They felt giddy. Even the dim light of a **medieval** cottage hurt their eyes. They could not sleep, and **diarrhea** set in. They felt dazed, and when they did manage to sleep, they went into a **delirium**, speaking rapidly and not making any sense.

Soon their groins and armpits began to break out in deep blue swellings (known as buboes), which itched with a tearing, cutting pain. Once this happened it would only be a matter of days before the victim died. At that time no one knew how to cure the plague. It was from these dark patches on the victims' bodies that the plague received its frightening nickname – the Black Death.

7

BEFORE THE PLAGUE

Country life

Most people in medieval Europe were **peasants**, living in the countryside in small villages. In England they usually owned some land of their own, but had to give up a lot of time to work on the land of the **lord of the manor**. This meant that they had to work very hard to grow a good crop on their own land. But they could not refuse to work for the lord; they even needed his permission before they could marry or leave the village.

Below *Peasants harvesting a wheat crop. This was done by hand, using tools called sickles.*

After a long day's work in the fields, peasants returned to their windowless huts. These were usually made of wood or mud, and had no furniture except a few stools and a rough table. Peasants' beds usually consisted of piles of straw. The whole family slept in one room, and the farm animals usually slept in there with them. Such houses were also "homes" for black rats. The rats lived in the straw and rubbish on the floor, or up in the **thatched roof**. People would not have bothered to get rid of the rats; after all, they helped to clean away unwanted scraps of food. No one had any idea that rats' fleas could give them the plague (see page 28).

Above *Life in Tarente, a typical fourteenth-century French town.*

Town life

If in 1349 you had climbed to the top of the tower of Bishop William's massive cathedral, the view would have been fairly typical of many small medieval towns all over Europe.

Towns were usually walled in to protect them from attack. Once you were through the town gate, you entered a maze of dirty, narrow, winding streets crowded with beggars and merchants, **friars** and **pilgrims**, soldiers and **jugglers**.

Open drains ran between the closely packed wooden houses. All kinds of garbage were poured into the drains, which flowed into the local river. The stench would have been overpowering, with rats, dogs and even pigs feeding off the garbage.

The Church

Religion played a very important part in people's lives in medieval times. Everyone was expected to attend church regularly and had to pay a tax of one tenth of their goods to the Church. The priest was usually the most knowledgeable person in a village and people looked to him to explain things they did not understand. When the plague struck, they turned to priests to explain what was happening and why. At first people thought that only wicked people caught the plague. Later events proved them sadly mistaken.

Below *The beautiful clothes worn by priests set them apart.*

Hunger and sickness

All over Europe, the population had increased rapidly during the thirteenth century. But the amount of food that was produced did not increase as fast. Since 1300, summers had become wetter and colder, causing poor harvests. This made the shortage even worse, sometimes causing **famine**.

Because people did not eat properly they became sick easily. So, in 1349, people who caught a serious illness, such as the plague, had little chance of surviving. There were no doctors with scientific training. **Physicians** and **apothecaries** offered cures, but often had no idea how to treat the patient. They usually bled their patients, or gave them herbs. These methods would have made no difference to the effects of plague, although in some cases they may have made an illness worse.

War

War was a common feature of life in medieval Europe. The life of a soldier was even harsher than that of a peasant. Large numbers of men never reached the battlefield; they died of disease before they got there. In 1337 a war started between England and France that was to become known as the Hundred Years War. By 1349, the plague was already in France, and English soldiers returning from France brought the plague with them.

Left *English soldiers attacking the French at the battle of La Roche in 1347.*

Right *A typical medieval street scene with all its color and its dirt. Can you find a rat in the picture?*

PLAGUE!

In the fourteenth century, the Italian town of Genoa was one of the busiest ports in Europe. Ships sailed from Genoa to trade all over the Mediterranean and into the Black Sea. Some goods were even shipped around the coast of Spain and France to England. Genoese merchants traded many goods from Asia such as spices, precious metals and silk. They did not know, however, that the plague had broken out in Asia and was fast spreading westward.

One of Genoa's main trading points with Asia was a town in the **Crimea** called Caffa (today it is called Feodosiya). The Mongols, a people who had been fighting their way across Asia since the twelfth century, realized how wealthy they would become if they captured Caffa. In 1347, the Mongol army attacked the town, battering its walls with huge stones fired from great wooden **catapults**, but the Genoese were determined to keep Caffa and refused to surrender.

Left *The impressive port of Genoa as it would have appeared at that time. Genoa's position in the center of the main trading route made it one of the busiest medieval ports.*

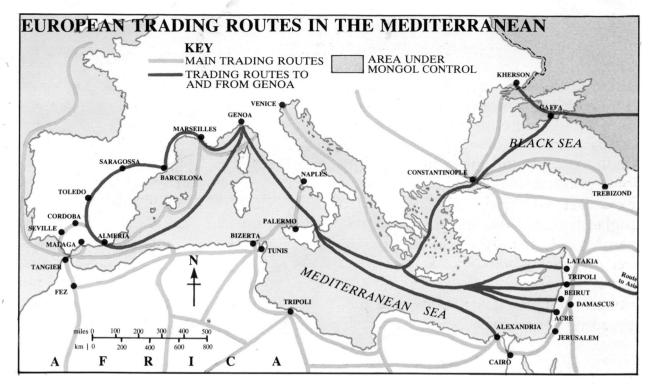

EUROPEAN TRADING ROUTES IN THE MEDITERRANEAN

KEY
— MAIN TRADING ROUTES
— TRADING ROUTES TO AND FROM GENOA
▢ AREA UNDER MONGOL CONTROL

KHERSON
CAFFA
BLACK SEA
VENICE
GENOA
MARSEILLES
CONSTANTINOPLE
TREBIZOND
SARAGOSSA
BARCELONA
NAPLES
TOLEDO
CORDOBA
PALERMO
SEVILLE
BIZERTA
MALAGA
ALMERIA
TUNIS
LATAKIA
TANGIER
TRIPOLI
Route to Asia
FEZ
BEIRUT
DAMASCUS
N
ACRE
MEDITERRANEAN SEA
TRIPOLI
ALEXANDRIA
JERUSALEM

miles 0 100 200 300 400 500
km | 0   200 400 600 800

A F R I C A
CAIRO

Above *The plague was spread quickly from one port to another by the rats that lived on ships. Soon many ports were affected, and the plague spread inland from there.*

Left *Fourteenth-century ships similar to those used by the Genoese.*

13

The **siege** went on for months, but eventually the Mongol commander Jannibeg Khan thought up a grim, but effective way of defeating the Genoese. Plague had struck in his army. There were many dead bodies and it was going to take a long time to bury them. There was a danger that the bodies might infect the rest of the army if they were left lying around. Jannibeg Khan ordered his men to use the catapults to fire the plague-infected bodies into the town. He hoped that the people in Caffa would catch the plague and so would be unable to hold off his army.

Jannibeg Khan's trick worked well. The plague took hold in the besieged town. However, it did not stop there. After the Mongols had taken Caffa, the Genoese ships continued their trade. Crews carrying goods back to Italy from Caffa took the plague with them. On some of the ships, every single member of the crew died at sea. When it became known that sailors on Genoese ships were suffering from the plague, Italian ports refused to allow them to enter. So they sailed to the southern coast of France instead.

Jannibeg Khan orders his soldiers to fire the plague-infected corpses over the walls of Caffa.

14

Plague in Europe

In December 1347, the plague broke out in Marseilles. From there it spread rapidly all over France. Because people had no idea how the plague was carried, they could not keep it from spreading. Rich and poor alike fell victim to it. In some places, rich people were able to escape the plague for a while, by moving away from an infected area. But eventually there was nowhere left to run to: every city, town and village was affected.

Wherever the Black Death took hold, at least one person in four died in dreadful pain. Sometimes all the people in a village or a town would be killed by the plague.

Above *The old section of the port of Marseilles as it is today.*

Below *With few exceptions the plague spread over all of Europe.*

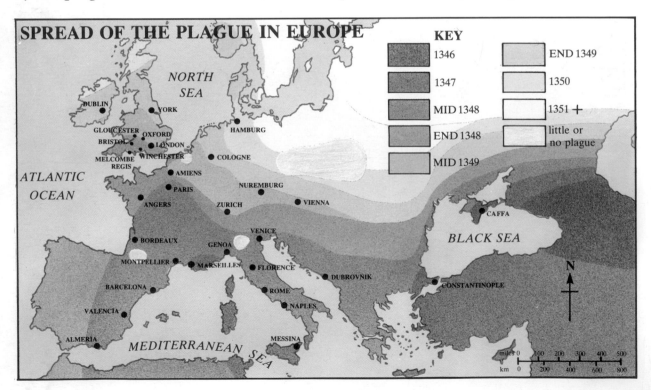

SPREAD OF THE PLAGUE IN EUROPE

KEY

1346	END 1349
1347	1350
MID 1348	1351 +
END 1348	little or no plague
MID 1349	

NORTH SEA

DUBLIN
YORK
GLOUCESTER OXFORD
HAMBURG
BRISTOL LONDON
MELCOMBE WINCHESTER
REGIS
COLOGNE
AMIENS
ATLANTIC OCEAN
PARIS
NUREMBURG
ANGERS ZURICH
VIENNA
CAFFA
BORDEAUX VENICE
GENOA
BLACK SEA
MONTPELLIER MARSEILLES
FLORENCE
BARCELONA
DUBROVNIK
ROME
CONSTANTINOPLE
VALENCIA
NAPLES
ALMERIA
MESSINA
MEDITERRANEAN SEA

N

miles 0   100   200   300   400   500
km 0   200   400   600   800

Plague in England

With the war continuing between France and England, it was only a matter of time before the same disaster hit England. The **chronicler** Geoffrey the Baker described its progress:

"At first it carried off almost all the inhabitants of the seaports in Dorset, and then those living inland, and from there it raged so dreadfully through Dorset and Somerset as far as Bristol. The men of Gloucester refused to allow people from Bristol into their region, as they all thought that the breath of those who lived amongst people who died of plague was infectious.

"But at last it attacked Gloucester, then Oxford and London, and finally the whole of England with such violence that scarcely one in ten of either sex was left alive. As there were not enough graveyards, fields were set aside for the burial of the dead."

Above *The Black Death as seen by an artist at the time. The central figure represents the plague, and the people who are hit by the arrows are the plague's victims.*

17

Flagellants thought that sin caused the plague (see page 26) and beat themselves to try to gain God's forgiveness. **Above** *In Germany and* **Right** *on a pilgrimage to Rome.*

Geoffrey the Baker's estimate of the number of people who died is much worse than modern historians have calculated (about three out of every four survived – see page 20). Perhaps the place where he lived was particularly badly affected. Certainly, burying people in ordinary fields was a desperate act. In the **Middle Ages**, most people believed that you would go to hell if you were not buried in a **consecrated** graveyard.

William Dene, a monk of Rochester, described the effect of the plague on one household:

"The Bishop of Rochester didn't keep many servants or **retainers**. Yet he lost four priests, five gentlemen, ten serving men, seven young clerks, and six **pages**, so that not a soul remained to serve him in any post . . .

Below *A medieval surgeon treating his patients. Treatments were crude and little could be done for those who were seriously ill, like plague victims.*

"During the epidemic, many chaplains and paid **clerics** would serve only if they were paid excessive salaries . . . priests hurried off to places where they could get more money than in their own **benefices** . . . . There was also so great a shortage of laborers and workmen of every kind in those days that more than a third of the land over the whole kingdom lay uncultivated."

Nothing, it seemed, could stop the plague; all people could do was pray they would not fall victim to it.

AFTERMATH

Population figures for the Middle Ages are not exact, so it is difficult to know how many people died of the Black Death before the **epidemic** stopped in the 1350s. However, it seems likely that over all of Europe at least one person in four died from it. In many places, the figure was much higher. It took generations, in some areas even centuries, for the population to recover. This was not helped by the fact that the plague did not just go away, but kept on returning. Figures for England in 1348 show a population of about 3.7 million; by 1377, this had dropped to about 2.2 million. In all of Europe between 1347 and 1351 about 25 million people died from the plague.

Life for the survivors

If, on average, only three people were left to do what had previously been the work of four, those three were at least in a position to try to bargain for higher **wages**. Governments passed laws fixing wages at the pre-plague levels, but often these laws were simply ignored.

Below *It took over 200 years for the population of England to recover.*

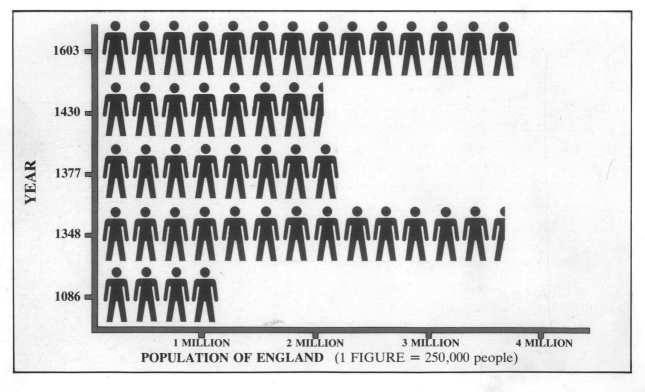

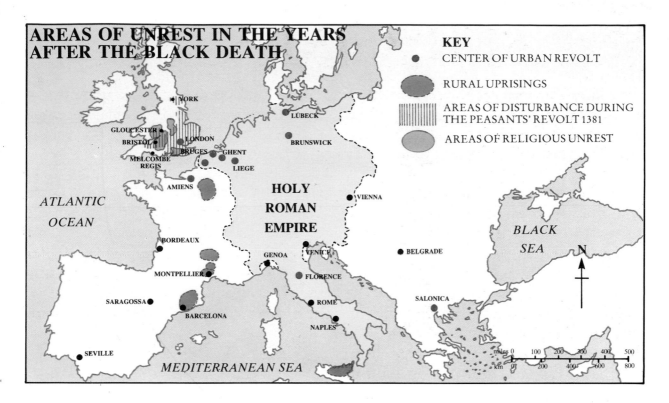

AREAS OF UNREST IN THE YEARS AFTER THE BLACK DEATH

KEY

● CENTER OF URBAN REVOLT

RURAL UPRISINGS

|||||| AREAS OF DISTURBANCE DURING THE PEASANTS' REVOLT 1381

AREAS OF RELIGIOUS UNREST

YORK

LÜBECK

GLOUCESTER
BRISTOL
LONDON
BRUGES GHENT
MELCOMBE REGIS
LIEGE

BRUNSWICK

AMIENS

HOLY
ROMAN
EMPIRE

VIENNA

ATLANTIC
OCEAN

BLACK
SEA

N

BORDEAUX

GENOA
VENICE

BELGRADE

MONTPELLIER

FLORENCE

SARAGOSSA

ROME

SALONICA

BARCELONA

NAPLES

SEVILLE

MEDITERRANEAN SEA

miles 0   100   200   300   400   500
km   0   200   400   600   800

The work had to be done, but people were not interested in working for wages well below what they knew they could get. In time, **employers** throughout Europe had to raise wages or go without the workers they needed.

In some places, there were simply not enough workers to keep a farm going. So, as farms failed, peasants who had earned a living by working on the land now drifted to the towns to try to find work. Those with land were often in a position to bargain for more. In England, if a community died out completely, **landlords** were able to take over the land for their own use. Often, nobody could stop them; those who might have done so were dead.

Above *There were many uprisings in Europe after the Black Death.*

Below *Threshing wheat. For some survivors, life returned to normal.*

21

Anger at priests and physicians

The Black Death seriously weakened the authority of the Church. Priests seemed to be powerless in the face of the epidemic. Some had shown cowardice as well, fleeing to save their own lives instead of looking after the victims. Many of those who had the courage to stay died with those that they were trying to help.

Physicians failed to find a treatment that made any real difference to those who had the plague. Their methods were laughed off and rejected.

"His cure for the plague only made me worse!" An apothecary (**Left**) faces the anger of the people his medicines have failed to cure.

Discontent

The plague naturally affected people's attitudes. Medieval people were used to misery and hunger, especially when bad weather ruined their crops or disease killed off their animals. They were even used to bands of soldiers burning their crops and looting their villages. But an epidemic on this scale was harsh even for them. People became reluctant to plan for the future, or to start any ambitious projects (such as Bishop William's project to rebuild Winchester cathedral).

When ordinary people saw the rich try to flee to safety while the poor had to stay put and await the plague's

Above *Rioting peasants loot a rich man's house during an uprising.*

arrival, they grew bitter and envious. That bitterness did not go away when the plague did, but remained, and in England it showed itself in the **Peasants' Revolt** of 1381. Years of discontent boiled over in this violent rebellion by ordinary people.

Although the Black Death had gone, the memory of it remained strong, and life did not go back to normal. Although the Peasants' Revolt was put down, the power of the lords never returned to what it had been in the days before the plague.

Above *The Court of the Exchequer was responsible for organizing the collection of the unpopular poll tax. Many people objected to having to pay this tax and revolted against the authorities.*

Left *The King of England, Richard II (on the boat), faces the rioting peasants.*

SEARCH FOR A CURE

Wherever the plague struck, people looked for a way of curing it. At first, the treatments were crude, but through trial and error, methods for controlling and even curing bubonic plague were eventually discovered.

Fourteenth-century "causes" and "cures"

Physicians at Paris University claimed that the stars had infected the sea, causing it to give off a vapor which fell as rain. The only way to protect yourself from this vapor was to light huge bonfires; then you had to make sure that you were not rained on, and that you did not use rain water for cooking.

In Switzerland people accused **Jews** of poisoning the water supplies. In one Swiss town every Jew was rounded up and burned to death. This was one of the saddest incidents during the Black Death. While millions of people were dying of the disease, healthy Jewish people lost their lives because of the fear and ignorance of others.

Some thought that God had sent the plague to punish people's wickedness. In Germany and eastern Europe, people wandered from village to village, whipping themselves mercilessly to show they were sorry. These flagellants, as they were called, were refused entry to many towns because of their violence and extreme views. This was sensible anyway because the flagellants themselves might have been infected with the plague.

Jews were rounded up in Basle, Switzerland, because they were accused of causing the plague by poisoning the water. They were put on a raft on the Rhine River and then burned to death. Notice the gold circle they had to wear to show that they were Jews.

The terror is tamed

In the centuries following the Black Death, bubonic plague continued to break out from time to time (as it did in London in 1664). The only action that proved effective against plague was to isolate infected people. This stopped the plague from spreading once it had broken out, but it did not help those who had already caught it.

In 1894, more than 500 years after the Black Death, Japanese and French scientists discovered the germ that caused the plague – a type of **bacteria**, which they named *Pasteurella pestis*. Over the following decade it was also discovered that the germ is transmitted by rats' fleas. The rats catch the plague

Above *The black rat. Its fleas spread the disease.*

Below *Wherever rats lived near people, the plague continued to spread.*

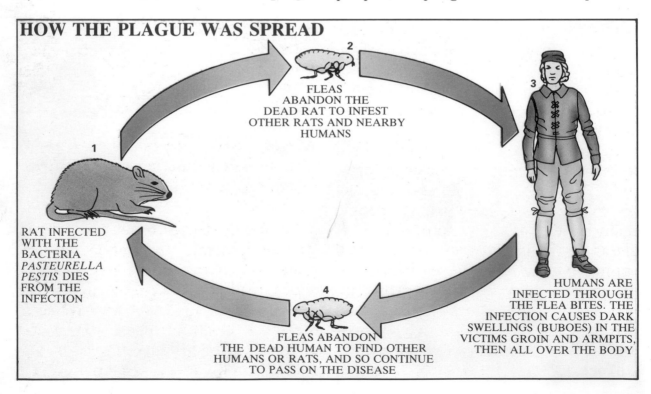

HOW THE PLAGUE WAS SPREAD

2. FLEAS ABANDON THE DEAD RAT TO INFEST OTHER RATS AND NEARBY HUMANS

3. HUMANS ARE INFECTED THROUGH THE FLEA BITES. THE INFECTION CAUSES DARK SWELLINGS (BUBOES) IN THE VICTIMS GROIN AND ARMPITS, THEN ALL OVER THE BODY

4. FLEAS ABANDON THE DEAD HUMAN TO FIND OTHER HUMANS OR RATS, AND SO CONTINUE TO PASS ON THE DISEASE

1. RAT INFECTED WITH THE BACTERIA *PASTEURELLA PESTIS* DIES FROM THE INFECTION

themselves, and like humans they usually die from it. When a rat dies, the fleas on it need to find a new host. However, when many rats have died there may not be any nearby for the fleas to feed on. If people are nearby they become the fleas' new hosts. When they are bitten by the fleas they also become infected with the plague.

Today, the plague can be cured if people are given antibiotics, medicines that destroy the bacteria that cause the disease. However, if rats or other **rodents** are prevented from **infesting** people's homes, then it is unlikely that anyone will catch the plague.

Even though bubonic plague can now be controlled, some people fear that the disease **AIDS** may soon become as damaging as the plague once was. Like the plague, it is **lethal** to those who catch it, and as with the plague in 1349, there is no cure. However, doctors know how AIDS is carried and how it can be avoided.

In fact, most of the diseases that used to kill thousands of people every year, such as smallpox and cholera, can now be avoided by **inoculating** people against them. If someone does catch a disease, modern medicine is well equipped to help. However, in some of the world's poorer countries, people are not always inoculated against such diseases, and so, even though we now know how to prevent them, epidemics still occur.

Above *A twentieth-century plague victim. Buboes can be seen just below his ear on his neck.*

Although there have been many terrible epidemics throughout history, none have been as long lasting, widespread or damaging as that which hit Europe in 1347. As we have seen, the Black Death changed every aspect of life in medieval Europe. It was perhaps the greatest disaster in history.

GLOSSARY

AIDS (Acquired Immune Deficiency Syndrome) A recently discovered disease that is fatal to people who catch it – doctors are still looking for a cure.

Apothecary A person who made a living by selling medicine, like druggists today.

Bacteria Tiny living bodies that can cause disease and decay.

Benefice A placement for a priest – for instance a parish. Some of the parish's income goes to the priest.

Bishop The head of a diocese. The diocese is the district, often very large, administered by a bishop from his cathedral.

Bubonic plague The form of plague that causes the sufferer to break out in buboes, or hard swellings. Until the twentieth century, a fatal epidemic disease.

Catapult A device for hurling objects. In the past, large catapults were used in war to throw huge boulders long distances.

Cathedral The main church in a district (or diocese), which acts as the bishop's headquarters.

Chronicler A person who writes down a history of events, or chronicle.

Clergy The priests and ministers of the Christian Church.

Cleric A member of the clergy.

Consecrate To make a place or building sacred or holy.

Crimea A peninsula on the north shore of the Black Sea.

Delirium The state of mind often caused by a fever, in which a person becomes restless and excited, and sees things that are not there.

Diarrhea An illness in which watery waste matter is passed frequently from a person's bowel.

Employer A person (or company) who provides people with paid work.

Epidemic An outbreak of a disease that many people in an area catch in a short space of time.

Famine A serious shortage of food throughout an area.

Friar A member of a religious order of the Roman Catholic Church. Friars lead a simple life and rely on gifts from the public for their living.

Infest To swarm over in a harmful way. The word usually refers to pests such as rats or fleas.

Inoculate To inject someone with a mild form of a disease so as to build up immunity to that disease.

Jew A person whose religion is Judaism.

Juggler An entertainer who throws and catches objects continuously, so that most of them are in the air at the same time.

Landlord A person who owns and rents out land or property.

Lord of the manor The person in charge of a village in medieval times.

Medieval Belonging to, or having to do with, the Middle Ages.

Middle Ages The period from the fifth to the fifteenth century.

Page A boy employed to run errands and carry messages.

Peasant One of the chiefly European or Asian class of people who work the land, usually as farm laborers.

Peasants' Revolt (1381) The rebellion in England when peasants protested to the king about the amount of tax that they were being forced to pay.

Physician A person who treats diseases.

Pilgrim Someone who makes a long journey to visit a holy place.

Plague See bubonic plague.

Population All the people living in a place (such as a country, or a city).

Retainer A type of servant.

Rodent A small mammal with sharp front teeth for gnawing. Rats, mice and squirrels are rodents.

Siege The surrounding of a city, fort, castle, etc. by an enemy army that is trying to capture it.

Symptom Something that shows you have a disease or illness of some kind.

Thatched roof A roof that is made of straw or reed.

Wage The money people are paid for working.

BOOKS TO READ

The Age of Chivalry: English Society 1200–1400 by Sylvia Wright (Warwick Press, 1988)

The Black Plague by Walter Oleksy (Franklin Watts, 1982)

For background information try:
Everyday Life in the Middle Ages by Fiona McDonald (Silver Burdett, 1985)

Growing Up in the Medieval Times by Penny Davies (David & Charles, 1980)

Older readers interested in a fictional treatment of the terrors of a plague epidemic (though not the Black Death itself) should read a translation of Albert Camus' *The Plague*.

INDEX

ACKNOWLEDGMENTS

The illustrations on pages 4–5, 11, 14–15, 22–3 and 26–7 are by Patrick Bullock. The illustrations on pages 13, 16, 20, 21 and 28 are by Peter Bull. The cover illustration is by Stephen Wheele, based on a medieval woodcut (the original of which was provided by Ronald Sheridan).

The publishers would like to thank the following for providing the photographs in this book: BBC Hulton Picture Library 12; Bruce Coleman 28; ET Archive 8, 9(b), 10, 18(b), 21, 24, 25(t); Mary Evans Picture Library 6, 9(t), 13, 25(b); Mansell Collection 18(t); Ronald Sheridan 7, 17, 19; Topham Picture Library 16, 29.